Sandalwood-Scented Skeletons

poems by

Rhea Dhanbhoora

Finishing Line Press
Georgetown, Kentucky

Sandalwood-Scented Skeletons

ACKNOWLEDGMENTS

In Diaspora: *Capsule Stories* Autumn 2020 Edition
Itemizing my Identity: *Capsule Stories* Autumn 2020 Edition
[also nominated for a Puschart Prize]
Collective Shame: *Capsule Stories* Autumn 2020 Edition
Home: Fly on the Wall Press, *Unite Magazine*
Categories we fit in: *The Lit Quarterly*

Publisher: Leah Huete de Maines
Editor: Christen Kincaid
Cover Art: Natasha Mistry
Author Photo: Michael LaChance
Cover Design: Elizabeth Maines McCleavy

Order online: www.finishinglinepress.com
also available on amazon.com

Author inquiries and mail orders:
Finishing Line Press
PO Box 1626
Georgetown, Kentucky 40324
USA

Table of Contents

IN DIASPORA

I

There are words people like me will hear that you don't know:
markers of our minority, snaking the slow growth of invisible identity.
Tandarosti, and I know to raise my glass. But I don't hear this
anymore;
it is not a country I have left behind but a colony on
the brink of extinction.
Khandia, I hear once as my grandfather is carried by corpse-bearers
to the
Dakhma: what we call the Tower of Silence, at the top of which lie the
lost bodies of our moribund community,
in concentric circles, waiting for vultures to feed on their flesh.

II

What, not who, you ask, is a Parsi. It's complicated: I explain—too
much, too little, not at all.
Long-nosed, elite, upper-class; refugees, marginalized, disappearing;
interesting, eccentric, hilarious; uninteresting, aberrant, unnecessary;
you represent us, you decide.

III

Choi we call the best type of tea: flavorful cups, black tea leaves boiled
to super-strength with lemongrass and mint, sometimes ginger;
it is *chai* not *choi*, you say in the country we now call home. But it is
not the same, this choi once brewed best by my grandmother who no
longer makes it, now in the Dakhma with my grandfather, I like to
think, though really some vulture carries their memories through the
sky in its belly.

IV

Applaud our congenial constitution; long-term sequelae of
displacement; diaspora lost in antiquities no longer studied.

V

Sometimes when I look up I wonder
if I will ever see the vultures again in waking life;
sky burials: you are horrified by the obsequies that bring me peace.

ITEMISING MY IDENTITY

There are many things I cannot do

Write well enough to sufficiently express outrage, for / against a
country I call home now sinking under the heavy weight of fascism
they will tell you does not exist; worry about my diaspora in despair
you do not know is quickly dying / dead; say it is unfair when family
members die living to a ripe old over-eighty because
how dare I / I have been lucky; travel because we are pandemic
stuffed / I am an alien lacking the luxury of reentry.

There are things I have done once that I will never do again

Climb mountains, reach the top shelf of the pantry, stand
several hours, breathe, walk, sleep without stenosis
slowly surging up and down my one-disc shy spine;
sit at the same table as grandfather, grandmother, great-
uncles, certain friends passed on to places I don't believe exist;
drive a small yellow car no longer mine.

There are things I try not to do
Succumb to anxiety attacks; take the things I have /
have had for granted;
be impatient, unkind; talk too much / too little of life in diaspora;
spend sleepless nights
wondering what if / how come / if only.

There are things
I have not; will not; can no longer even try.

There are things
Still here, once around, never seen, now gone,
always part of me.

YOU, ME, US PARSI'S PASSING ON

Pick a place to watch the beginning of the end.

Perhaps there will be ceremonies, and we'll watch from front-row seats.

Soak up the easy scent of rosewater, see lilies lining the sides of the halls, sniff deeper to inhale all the musk and sandalwood rising up— whiffs of smoke from the last-rites that doesn't smell the same as it used to.

Soft, symbolic muslin, slipping slowly through our fingers.

A low hum: bass tones, a baritone: flitting out of a hidden room: those tables set, decorated: the food, flowers, bodies—ready to be devoured.

A lilting melody wafting over, the sweet smell of pudding, roasts and alcohol—it's all waiting, watching as we dwindle.

Dawn slips into dusk as we go from 61,000 down to 60,000 down to…

On the table: sandalwood, musk, rosewater, wilted lilies.

Soon, no sign
—of us—of me—of you.

COLLECTIVE SHAME

So embarrassing. Today is another rarest of rare occurrence: one of us is in the news. For days the gated spaces will be filled with gray heads, the tittle-tattlers of the community reigniting once-flushed fires. Noses wrinkled, heads bowed, friends in the press calling, emailing *have you heard* even though of course we've heard, how could we not? What it's about doesn't matter: a small fight in a private space, misallocation of funds, another of those recent orthodox versus modern arguments over what Zarathustra thought of conversions though we all know no prophet really wrote the scriptures. It's the tag at the beginning of the name, the idea that this model minority has slipped, fallen from grace, not really schadenfreude but close even among our own. *Do you know them* because of course we do, like some exotic, near-extinct creature who knows by name, location, and personality every other of its kind; we *want* to say but cannot because so often we do know them, these "fallen" members of a maladjusted minority struggling for space but so ashamed of falling into the wrong one.
The failure of the one our failure too.

ROOM 52
[at The British Museum]

At the top of the East stairs they cast slices of a history
I call mine even though I will never really know it intimately.

Survey these replicas of the Hall of a Hundred Columns,
they tell me, explain the Palaces of Darius and Xerxes,
those ancient kings we still name our children after though
we say their palaces were in Persepolis in Persia
although they are not *wrong* when they write Iran.

In Room 52: they call it Ancient Iran though to me
this is Persia: they place the objects from this mighty Empire
now forgotten, those famous Achaemenid relics: Cyrus Cylinder
proudly encased behind glass I yearn to slip my fingers
through and caress, golden curve over golden curve over
golden curve...

In the West they keep our Eastern treasures: amulets, coins,
those crude model chariots so impressively soldered together,
those gorgeous griffin-headed bracelets—
who wore them what did they do, did they look like me?—
more glass to protect those Oxus Treasures we do not own
but once lived in the same land as,
though so far back I can no longer count...

SOME WOMEN YOU DON'T KNOW

You know the names; Cyrus, Xerxes, Darius;

the specifics don't matter.

You know them with crowns and accolades and empires,
or as those vague figures, some men from the East
once famous for doing saying being whatever those people
from that side of the world do say are, all shoved into one box
of history irrelevant to you. The East, I'm told
as I'm leered at paid less put down disappeared—
never was any kind of place for a woman.

You do not know Mandana, unless it is as mother of a man
whose declaration of human rights you display so proudly
in your museums.

You do not know Pantea Arteshbod, even as you see those
Western versions of her Immortal Army so lazily splashed
across your screen.

You do not know Cassandane,
unless you read between the lines of Herodotus' Histories
of that place too far too unfamiliar to really matter.

You do not know Artemisia I of Caria, except as another
skewed story with a pretty white face on your screens
meant to resemble ours.

I know more than you know but still I do not really know either;
I know only, as I am leered at paid less put down disappeared,
that although possibly fairer to my kind even if all accounts are
wrong,
the East—was once no worse a place for women
than here, now, this.

CATEGORIES WE FIT IN

fallow—
that is unsown, unseeded, dormant, barren: all best suited
to discuss land and time and such.
Yet so accurately also, its definition denotes
the current state of an ethnoreligious minority
that you know nothing of: though I would not use it to do so.

Fallow—
that is pretty antlered animals of the Old World, light brown coats
interrupted by white dots, the subspecies I mean, Persian fallow
hidden behind tall blades of grass: best categorised as near-extinct.
Yet so accurately also, its status describes the current state of
an ethnoreligious minority
that you now wonder about: though I would not use it to do so.

OUR VULTURES, VANISHED

Diclofenac—for your migraine, keratoses, livestock—
not for me.

My body, waiting for The Tower of Silence, cannot ingest
what you say exterminates the venerated Gyps that circle
the concentric rings at the top of the structure where our
lost lives once lay—perhaps still lie if rumors are to be
believed—tired bones poking through decayed flesh—
the skeletons we do not hide in the folds of plush-lined
funeral pillows or place on pyres—simply offer them
to the Gyps in our sky burials—to you so indecorous.

The Gyps will not have my flesh—diclofenac-loaded livestock
innocent—all culpability of death on those moribund people—like
me, you say.

HOME

At home inside—caged, confined, closeted; no, happily nestled—in a circular space like the concentric top of those Towers where we bury the dead, but this we call a colony; at home where we are happiest and we know all our neighbours; the doors always open, sandalwood-scented air everywhere, food flowing in-and-out-in-and-out—always home

In the monsoon—the scent of *boomla*, anhydrous Bombay Duck parched so prettily strung out on the promenades by the sea; that fishy odour you turn your nose up at and we sniff in like pleasant perfume; softened in ground chili-tomato pastes and coated in gram flour, cooked, fried, devoured—the open doors compounding its fragrance

At home outside—instructions for the proper way to assimilate—a mix of celebration and condescension, some bitterness but mostly indifference now; that funny thing where invisible is better than seen but also not really; hostile-hospitable-hostile-hospitable maybe we're crazy for thinking otherwise either way—still home

In the summer—sticky intrusions, the humidity mashing folds of skin together; that menacing warmth from the soughing of the wind spreading slowly—long, dry sweat-seasoned city streets hot to the touch, only welcome moisture that saccharine yellow pulp sometimes slightly tangy, squeezed from pliable skin all shades of green-yellow-orange; our lace curtains dotted with sun-baked dust still sparkling—steamy excuses for slumber

At home overseas—on whatever transoceanic journey, dissertation handy—in anticipation of questions, in search of community, at home alone; some days easier than others and still so appealing, that draw of the unknown; hostile-hospitable-hostile-hospitable maybe success is right around the corner—someday home

In the winter—fabricating snow, still just sticky mud; no hoarfrost just moderate breeze slightly better than the sticky-sweet summers—strawberries scuttled into synthetic boxes sold on the street, more straw than berry in those heavy boxes sold at red signals; the coldest months still not so cold in that archipelago, city once home now so far away; breeze-whisked leaves lining pavements, spilling out of rain-stained gutters—brief respite from sultrier seasons

TRANSITORY RAPPORT

Our encounter outside the elevator—
Like so many others in this small space we've made our own
where other people just like us huddle together
in small flats with lace curtains—
but so different because here you are at 3am,
Trembling alone, bent over, brain softened, searching
 for a cafeteria but no, really, for something familiar.

Connected by that apologetic caducity—
In two months my smile fading
In concert with yours.

ODDITIES ABOUT TOWN

They said what do you think about those oddities
leaving their dead to rot out in the open
as vulture-snacks;
letting that sandalwood fire
go to waste in a censer
—what do you think of those oddities

Silk scarf stinking of sandalwood,
swaying pretty to
hide the smile on my odd face.

HER PAINTINGS

In the home I no longer live in
that is, the home I left for this home I have now
—I think often of the table that keeps my grandmother alive.

The only tangible heirloom of the artist,
a bygone era memorialized by this oil-splashed
yellow orb that cushions Zarathustra's curly locks held down
by priestly white cap so carefully brushed in
—blues browns grays blacks whites in that one line to say
here, there was a slight crease and there, another fold.
Hint of robe, blot of sky, finger raised to heaven,
soft brown eyes staring as if to say don't worry, she lives, breathes in
this inspired
concoction of oils and turpentine
—my grandmother's hands once touched, felt, worked, reworked the
canvas
Her spirit now interwoven in the threads underneath its coated surface.

In the home I no longer visit
that is, the home she left for nonexistence
—I think often of the attic that holds more of my grandmother.

Piled one on top of the other little artifacts of the artist
I once knew but both no longer within grasp
one turned to dust the others locked away because I am told but do
not agree
they belong to someone else.

Canvas and custodian all out of reach perhaps I will never again
see, hold, touch another fabric once touched, felt, worked, reworked
—by my grandmother's hands.

MY MONA LISA

Enter this muted extent, room within room in the cloister of memories
within which I pretend I've seen this woman

plucked from some distant native Empire long-forgotten now preserved
in daubs, smears, the precise brush-strokes of a realist

In her dark element, lips pursed, slight upturn reaching eyes turned
away not towards the face of her own/my/your identity

my Mona Lisa so similar yet somehow more sombre, stygian gloom
eclipsed only by pearls snaking three times over flesh and fabric

Imagine those fingers working overtime over yards of whatever
material cotton/georgette/silk she is wrapped up in

Bordering her sari a symbol of syncretism, the hand-stitched *kor*—
intricate brocade, floral vines twisting and turning—affixed to the
edges of diaphanous fabric

Enter this quotidian scene suddenly so empty of and still filled with
singularity, peculiarity, originality—call her identity what you will

You know Leonardo I know Pestonji but I do not really *know* him—
like much else in what they call the western-realistic "Portrait of a Parsi
Lady," who I know and don't know

much like myself.

ALL OF US OVER THE CLIFF

In my dreams we're all floating,
balled up into a single angry cloud aware but yet unaware,
rising but still falling,
slipping in and out of global consciousness,
amaranthine wounds tearing at the seams,
necrotizing fasciitis of our decline snaking its way through the once
plump flesh of our community—the bacteria is us—you and me,
killing the soft tissue of our selfhood
slowly, slowly,
slipping into obscurity.

THIS FAITH, IMPIOUS

When I tell you I am not religious it is because I do not really believe
                                                    in what I cannot prove
Still I find comfort in the image of Zarathustra on my dressing table
My eyes light up when I smell the sandalwood in the silver afargans,
My muslin sudra is lovingly handled, safe in a special drawer—no
                                                    longer worn

still, I find comfort in the image of Zarathustra on my dressing table
Even though I do not pray, have not prayed in years
my muslin sudra is lovingly handled, safe in a special drawer—no
                                                    longer worn
But how can you love, celebrate, respect—if you do not worship?

Even though I do not pray, have not prayed in years
my eyes light up when I smell the sandalwood in the silver afargans.
But how can you love, celebrate, respect—if you do not worship?
When I tell you I am not religious it is because I do not really believe
                                                    in what I cannot prove

HISTORIES

When you think of your 'roots' do you think of the same things we do?

Compendium of traditions, ceremonies
From found fragments of lost histories?

Contested tales of bleeding rivers,
The blinding lights of conquest?

Empty, ravaged homes with crushed faiths
Running, racing, rowing to freedom?

When you think of your history,
What do you think of, know, love, celebrate, grieve, remember, forget?

AAPRO FREDDIE

You know when you *claim* someone and maybe they know, maybe they don't, and maybe they agree and maybe they don't but it doesn't really matter because there's no way you're going to fall out of love with this person who is *you* but also not you but someone else; bigger, brighter.

The thing is, we see him everywhere we don't usually see ourselves, and then we see ourselves in him so there we are, all of us: on stage, on your dusty vinyls and cassette tapes and broken CDs and in your heart and carved into your buildings and chiseled onto street corners.

He is everyone's and no one's, this four-octave rock God; immutable energy infecting Lake Geneva, that bronze body poised in eternal triumph, private loves, public personas: all of it mixed in with the sempiternal genius of his creations.

So when we say aapro which you don't understand and just nod and smile and think: *oh, there's another crazy Queen fan my gosh they got to the developing countries too,* and when you think of him as the hot, hot, hot British superstar, remember that was him, yes, most certainly—but for us, he is always *aapro* Freddie, that is: *our* Freddie.

Freddie from a city called Bulsar; Freddie who wore the white vests: *no coincidence they look so much like our Parsi sudras,* we like to joke; Freddie with those Parsi teeth and that distinct nose and the mustache that looks exactly like all the cool uncles swilling hard liquor at our weddings and Navjotes; Freddie with the big voice that told us without meaning to tell us that we could do it too.
Our Freddie.

UNFAMILIAR, FAMILIAR TERRITORY

Mention where we come from and we feel the sands of time slipping
                                          between our toes,
All these melodramatic waves washing up against a shore we can
picture but have never really seen, because we know it no longer
exists as we like to think of it.

Histories, memories, fabrications stepping in for the
Documents of a past that no longer exist in totality.

Heady back and forth between scholar and student gets faster, swirls
higher—reaches forward—except we're also the subject.

If we squint we can sketch out an imagined past: dusk drawn in
                                          hyper-lapse,
time crawling for the last rotation to let it all really soak into our false
                                          reminiscing.

The sun in the land we come from,
we hear,
trails through rich grains of sand
that turn from yellow to gold.

We hear, we read, perhaps we visit
—but we do not really know.

Drop a little more information into this yearning for ties to the
                                          homeland,
let us sit in it a while longer.

Take a trip to the edge of this ancient kingdom with us—here in the
past where our ancestors watched the ocean breeze from the coasts
and let little gold flecks settle on the tip of their dorsal humps.

We no longer belong where we come from, but once,
or so we hear,
there were a people there,
so much like us.

STEALING SPACE

Perhaps one day we will be known
As more than just a minority; described with words other than
Rare, exotic, eccentric, invisible.
So some future generation will be able to
Identify, categorize, classify us as more than a

Zealous minority: some *trying* to be different others *accepting*
                              they're not, with long noses and
Out-of-date traditions like those archaic Tower funeral practices
                                                          that
Really don't have any place in what they often call
Our country as if to clearly distinguish between
A majority who belongs and a minority who doesn't.
Still, how can we complain, any of us little groups so
Tenderly handled, inspired to assimilate, children no longer
Recognizing, desiring, any ties to these old identities
I speak of so often in this loud,
Annoying manner; just making up stories when really,
No one needs more space than they already have, do they?

FINAL QUESTIONS

What happens to bones left to air-dry in the sun?
Without the cushy blanket of soil, decomposition delayed
How quickly will sandalwood-scented skeletons turn to dust?
The cadaveric ecosystem hard at work under the skin,
even as soft tissue, dainty organs, flesh, bone all succumb
slowly to that permanent cessation; *lived-out, done.*

What covers your corpses when your body is done?
Ours roll over in muslin, fine-fabric in which to meet sun
and rain, fine-fabric in which to rest as bodies succumb
to the slow air-drying, up in the Tower where a delayed
putrefaction seeps in and rots soft tissue, skin,
dainty organs, flesh, bone—*all soon nothing but dust.*

The sandalwood-scented skeleton too, must turn to dust
—mustn't it? Lying on that hot concrete; lived-out, done,
evaporating with the memories once alive, now just skin
and bones, and not even skin once the sun
has played its sizzling part in this delayed,
but hastened decomposition; *all skeletons eventually succumb*

Does anyone really think of how the skeletons succumb
when their relatives are slowly turning to dust,
their grief hitting corpse-less patches of earth, delayed
distress striking long after funeral-rites are done?
Wrapped up in tears, who's looking up at the sun
thinking; it all succumbs: *flesh, bone... that pretty skin*

Gruesome, all these grisly thoughts of delayed
decomposition and the rotting of bone and skin,
Macabre talk of lives lived-out, dead, dying, done,
of those sandalwood-scented skeletons that succumb,
and how in graves, pyres, or concrete rings, we're all the same
                              dust, but only some of us;
in the Tower, in the sun.

Forget for a minute the bodies and their states of delayed
Decomposition; think of the smoky aromas on the skin
of these skeletons before the funeral rites are halfway done
The fragranced wood so strong, muslin is forced to succumb,
to let in hit after hit of heady aroma, encompassing the dust
long after; *and then the skeletons are placed outside, in the sun!*

Before that delayed rot strikes and the bodies succumb,
some skin is sandalwood-scented, transforms its skeletal dust
into sweet, smoky, sun-kissed drafts before *it's all done.*

WITH THANKS

It's impossible to name every incredible person who has influenced, inspired and motivated me through this collection and beyond. You know who you are, but to hover over you vaguely for a minute:

To my family, of course—those still with us, and those we've lost—who I do and do not write about and around, who inspire, encourage and motivate me every day, no matter how impractical what I decide to do seems in the moment.

To my partner, who has been living and breathing my stories and ideas with me for so long now that each little success feels like a joyous, shared experience.

To old friends back home, new friends here, to those I've been inspired by and continue to be inspired by in class and out of it, friends with whom I've read and shared work, my little community of writers and artists without whom I would not be half as inspired to put these words out anywhere. To those I speak with rarely but intimately, to all of you who know all the things about me that I keep hidden from everyone else.

To the professors and authors who pushed me and inspired me and continue to stay in touch and push me and inspire me, and to the publishers, readers and editors who have worked and read with me, published me, blurbed my book, invited me to readings and events, and allowed me to participate and engage in literary spaces.

I love and am grateful for you all.

After living most of her life in a cacophonous-yet-cherished city, Rhea now lives in relative quietude in Upstate New York with her partner and the cutest cat in the world.

She worked as an editor and writer in India for close to a decade, before quitting her job and moving to New York to finally write what everyone told her no one would read.

Her work has appeared or is forthcoming in various publications including *Chronogram, Peripheries Journal, Broccoli Mag, Capsule Stories, Five on the Fifth, The Spill, Malarkey Books* and *JMWW*. She's currently an editor at NutriSense, on the Board for literary organization, Quiet Lightning, and is working on several projects, among which is a linked collection of stories about women based in the underrepresented Parsi Zoroastrian diaspora.

Sandalwood-Scented Skeletons is her first chapbook. Follow her work at rheadhanbhoora.com.

CPSIA information can be obtained
at www.ICGtesting.com
Printed in the USA
BVHW031804110222
628354BV00002B/78